GW00383886

SONNETS FOR THE GODLY
& THE DAMNED

SONNETS FOR THE GODLY & THE DAMNED

... a handbook for the cocky sonneteer ...

Bill Homewood

Mimosa Books
1 Castle Banks
Lewes BN7 1UZ
www.mimosabooks.eu

© *Individual poems: Bill Homewood 2019*

© *This collection: Mimosa Books 2019*

ISBN: *9781791656782*

ALL RIGHTS RESERVED

This book contains material protected under International and Federal Copyright Laws and Treaties. Any unauthorized reprint or use of this material is prohibited. No part of this book may be reproduced or transmitted in any form or by any means, electronic or mechanical, including photocopying, recording, or any information storage and retrieval system, without written permission from the publisher

Cover: « Flower Queue » by Simon Menzies

iv

... for Claire Menzies ...

CONTENTS

… FOREWORD …

I am hoping that you, my reader, are a poet who has not yet written a sonnet, and that by the time you get to my last page you will be inspired to have a go. I have illustrated the book with 3 sonnets by Shakespeare and some gripes and joys of my own.

Fitting a thought or story into 14 lines, following a set rhyming scheme and a rhythmical form, is enjoyable for the writer; it can be a bit of a tussle, but the discipline enforces invention and economy. It is worth the scrap; the best art is often born of a huge fight with a limiting medium or an exacting convention. Think of the restrictions visited on the composer writing for orchestra and singers; and yet how magnificent the result can be.

You will know that there are several kinds of sonnet, mostly written in pentameter, with varying prescribed rhyming schemes: the Italian (or Petrarchan), the Spenserian, the Miltonic, the English (or Shakespearian), and variations. I especially like the English sonnet: 3 quatrains of alternating rhyme and a decisive final couplet. 14 lines is a nice length - it just gives you time to broach an idea, explore it a little and come to a cocky conclusion.

Being such a succinct medium, sonnets are ideal vehicles for irony, for paying compliments, or for expressing thoughts which, spoken eye to eye, would have you stammering.

In a sonnet, you can follow your heart for twelve lines, and use your head in the last two.

Bill Homewood

THE BIG STUFF

Sonnets can be witty, they can be ecstatic, they can be reflective, they can be angry. They are the perfect vehicle for a polemic, for an encapsulation of strong thoughts. They can be a cryptic game. They can be like miniature stage-plays, with plot, dramatic argument and dénouement.

The sonnet format acts as a template, forcing the writer to default to precision, to whittle away at a poem until it is lean and just right. Within this framework you can write without indulgence about the big subjects - love, death, philosophy - those subjects we ask our parents about, and our children ask us about, as we gaze together, in tiny community, at the great starry sky on a clear night...

A CONSUMMATION AND A DREADFUL BEAUTY

Earth labours through a rubble-spattered space,
Tired of turning, sick of its ugly load,
Towards an inevitable crash in some black place,
Some Armageddon on the stellar road,
The snap extinction of this Hell on Earth,
The snuffing-out of hatred, murder, loss,
A celestial blink, no more, to mark the birth
Of nothingness. As we blind-eyed the toss
Of Fate, the "heads we lose" – oh we lost our heads
Alright – so Time contemptuously spits
On triumphs, babies born and newly-weds,
On diners under the bridge and at the Ritz.

   To spin the tale to the end, Time's careless duty;
   A consummation and a dreadful beauty.

I like to mess with the convention, and devise my own schemes within the fourteen lines. The poet Stephen Spender read my heartbroken airport farewell IN AN AEROPLANE, AFTER SANTA BARBARA. He liked it very much because I had put the sonnet in a dramatic context by wrapping it with some free verse.

Over a glass of wine, he pronounced, "Of course, it's not strictly a sonnet, is it, Bill?" At the time, he was teaching a poetry class in the English Department at the University of Texas in Houston, and I was teaching a poetry class in the Theatre Department of the same university. By coincidence both of us were teaching sonnets that week.

You may agree with Stephen, and the poem certainly isn't an English Sonnet: In the sonnet section of the poem I have divided my 14 lines into 3 sections: 2 stanzas of 6, before the final couplet. However, the 5th and 6th lines of the second stanza are delayed rhymes with the 5th and 6th lines of the first stanza. It seems neat to me. I cordially invite the reader to call this a "Homewoodian" Sonnet!

IN AN AEROPLANE, AFTER SANTA BARBARA

Below,
A grey-blue skin
Shifts over earth's bone,
And under the leathery meniscus
Dumb whims
Make life and death simple.

As bark is split and in its mending lips
A pipping bud is bound against the sap,
And ancient shoots are trimmed with shorter tips
To draw the richer juices from the tap,
So you were joined to me in rooted love
And stirred the sleeping sugars of my mind.

While sporting buds were nipped within and died,
And erstwhile vital blooms unsuccoured fell,
And old spurs withered at the heel, denied
The nourishment from my beloving well,
Engorged, I felt you soak and swell above
My unstemmed stem, and share my blood in kind!

But now the graft is torn from this empire,
The stock is savage and reverts to briar.

Beyond the sea,
I think you are sad too,
Fading,
Where love was.

SONNETS IN PERFORMANCE

Shakespeare uses rhyme sparingly and deliberately in his plays, which are mostly written in blank verse. ROMEO & JULIET'S first meeting in I v is a strict sonnet. The lovers' instant empathy, and, especially, Juliet's quick wit, are obvious in their sharing of 14 structured, rhyming lines.

Romeo:
If I profane with my unworthiest hand
This holy shrine, the gentle sin is this:
My lips, two blushing pilgrims, ready stand
To smooth that rough touch with a tender kiss.

Juliet:
Good pilgrim, you do wrong your hand too much,
Which mannerly devotion shows in this;
For saints have hands that pilgrims' hands do touch,
And palm to palm is holy palmers' kiss.

Romeo:
Have not saints lips, and holy palmers too?

Juliet:
Ay, pilgrim, lips that they must use in prayer.

Romeo:
O, then, dear saint, let lips do what hands do;
They pray, grant thou, lest faith turn to despair.

Juliet:
Saints do not move, though grant for prayers' sake.

Romeo:
Then move not, while my prayer's effect I take.

In Shakespeare's LOVE'S LABOUR'S LOST V ii, Berowne makes a plea for prosaic, honest wooing ("russet yeas, and honest kersey noes"). He attacks effete poetical lovers who woo "in rhyme" with "Taffeta phrases, silken terms precise".

O, never will I trust to speeches penned,

Nor to the motion of a schoolboy's tongue,

Nor never come in visor to my friend,

Nor woo in rhyme, like a blind harper's song.

Taffeta phrases, silken terms precise,

Three-piled hyperboles, spruce affectation,

Figures pedantical - these summer flies

Have blown me full of maggot ostentation.

I do forswear them, and I here protest,

By this white glove - how white the hand, God knows! -

Henceforth my wooing mind shall be expressed

In russet yeas, and honest kersey noes.

And to begin, wench, so God help me, la!

My love to thee is sound, sans crack or flaw.

Ha! Good old Shakespeare! The joke's on Berowne: the speech itself is a strict, rhyming sonnet! The very weapon of choice for the precious, affected, courtly lovers he is deriding!

Whether it be in a play or a recital, the driving engine for the sonnet in performance is the metre. For the performer it is more effective to count the metrical feet than the syllables, just as the musician counts the basic unit of rhythm in a composition: 3/4, 4/4, 6/8, whatever.

It is often said that Shakespeare wrote his verse in Iambic Pentameter. Take it from me, this is not strictly true. It would be better to put it like this: aside from the four-square doggerel he used for witches, fairies and clowns, he wrote his verse in pentameter, which is often, but <u>not always</u>, iambic.

*How ugly and unnatural it would be to deliver the first line of Shakespeare's Sonnet 18 in iambs: Shall <u>I</u> com<u>**pare**</u> thee <u>**to**</u> a <u>**Summ**</u>er's <u>**day**</u>? Only announcers over train station tannoys emphasize prepositions like that: "Passengers are advised to go <u>**to**</u> Platform 9…"*

The performer will choose a scansion, nonetheless finding 5 metrical feet in each line (as the musician will find 5 quarter-notes in a 5/4 measure). The options include:

*Shall <u>I</u> com<u>**pare**</u> <u>**thee**</u> to a <u>**summ**</u>er's <u>**day**</u>?*
*Shall <u>I</u> com<u>**pare**</u> thee ^ to a <u>**summ**</u>er's <u>**day**</u>?*
*Shall <u>I</u> com<u>**pare**</u> thee to a <u>**summ**</u>er's <u>**day**</u>? ^*

SONNET 18

Shall I compare thee to a summer's day?

Thou art more lovely and more temperate.

Rough winds do shake the darling buds of May,

And summer's lease hath all too short a date.

Sometime too hot the eye of heaven shines,

And often is his gold complexion dimmed;

And every fair from fair sometime declines,

By chance, or nature's changing course, untrimmed;

But thy eternal summer shall not fade,

Nor lose possession of that fair thou ow'st,

Nor shall death brag thou wand'rest in his shade,

When in eternal lines to Time thou grow'st.

    So long as men can breathe, or eyes can see,

    So long lives this, and this gives life to thee.

I wrote ALL LOVED-UP AT THE HOLY SEPULCHRE with performance in mind. I had dined out on this adventure a few times over the years, and played for my laughs over a bottle or two of wine with much acting-out and attention to timing. Hmm. Reducing a ten-minute anecdote to three concise sonnets was a salutary exercise.

In 1977 Estelle and I performed with the Royal Shakespeare Company at the Jerusalem Festival. On an afternoon off, we wandered in the spicy air of the Old City. We bargained with traders, sipping their sweet mint tea; we dodged the butchers' stalls and admired the carpets. One day we fell in with a sweating group of trouser-bursting, cross-toting pilgrims from the American Mid-West, who were heading for the Holy Sepulchre. With them, we discovered the bizarre Coptic monastery, a series of tiny huts on the roof of the Holy Sepulchre, where thin Ethiopian monks, blanketed against the heat, sat about in silence on the stone buttresses and low walls.

One of the monks invited us to visit their chapel...

ALL LOVED-UP AT THE HOLY SEPULCHRE

"God loves you," lisped our host, and cast our coins
Like silver seed a-tinkle in a tray;
Some star-struck born-againers from Des Moines,
By a ghostly monk were shooed away
Down an ancient stairwell to our right,
In single file, their Nikes stroking stone,
All hush, all awe; a creak, a crash of light,
A thudding door - and we were quite alone.
He sidled close, his arm-bone clamped my waist,
He wheezed the scent of tombs up at my face,
Our elfin, bearded, toothless Coptic priest,
And us, all loved-up in this holy place.

    He drew us to the disappearing stair,
    A shade enticing victims to his lair.

The bone was tightening; this was not much fun,
I wish I'd guessed the end he had in mind;
The stair so narrow Elf and I were one,
We followed you, four shuffling feet behind,
The vault crepuscular, sickly the air;
Our guide, rheumatic in old hessian shoes,
Toeing the dust to test each well-rubbed stair,
A dwarfish incubus I could not lose.
The door at last. His right hand snaked to pull
It wide, his lizard left hand found an in,
And as he shoved us through he plundered all,
My balls, my willy, all my private skin,

And we were out, the door behind us slammed,
Defiled amongst the godly and the damned.

Our laughter was a desecration, though

The Holy Sepulchre's a comic place,

With legion bleeding Mary's stabbed quite through,

And pendant Jesu's daft, lugubrious face.

A soldier ordered us to leave the square,

And off we scrambled, shamed down to our shoes,

To the Via Dolorosa, where

A simpering Christian maiden waved Good News:

A picture of two stick men, one behind

Akimbo, and the legend truly read

In kiddy's font: "The blind leading the blind"!

At this point you and I were screaming dead.

    "God loves you," said the godly girl He'd sent,

    And We were glad, and damned, and off We went.

CRAZY, WHATEVER is another "Homewoodian" sonnet, in which lines 5 and 6 rhyme with lines 11 and 12. This time I made it even harder for myself with the rhyming scheme ABABCD; ABABCD; EE. Once again I have bookended the sonnet with free verse.

In my collection UNDER THE BLUE (Mimosa Books 2015) I introduced this poem as follows...

In April 2003, at full gallop, my big grey Lusitano, Aston, had some sort of crisis on a grassy mountain top in the Languedoc. I was looking to the left, and never saw what it was that spooked him. He skidded to a dead stop in a second, reared and pirouetted so violently that I was thrown by centrifugal force, my foot trapped in the stirrup.

The next thing I knew I was being dragged down the side of the mountain at forty miles per hour. Aston was fleeing for the farm by the direct route. The scrubby, stony Garrigue shot by like background to a fast tracking shot as I bounced from rock to rock. Before I lost consciousness, I thought to myself: "This must look amazing!"

They got me to the polyclinique at Ganges. I'd broken and ruptured just about everything breakable and rupturable in my body, including 15 ribs. My torso was like a bag of loose coat-hangers. A week later, emerging from a morphine-induced trance in which even the plainest little old nurse had looked like a goddess of love, I wrote CRAZY, WHATEVER for Estelle.

CRAZY, WHATEVER

I always, whatever the game,
Carried my world, all of it, in a flight bag,
Ready for whatever,
Alone with the game,
Flying solo,
Always,
Until you.

The game's a high-risk sport, a crazy dash,
A hand of cards, a freefall jump, a shot
Through war-skies, strobing probes, each killing slash
All white, so white, our screaming wings white-hot
Or ice-cold black, or gone, each hop or skip
Or jump a dance of chance, a throw, a pot.

The path careers and swings towards a crash
That's set. We both know this I think, but not
The timing, nor the peace or pain. The hash
God makes we make – yes, we are God; we got
Our wings at birth, but no flight plan. We flip
A card, pass through some doors, to fly or rot.

And knowing what we don't want helps us choose.
The game's in the bag, my love, we just can't lose.

Since you,
My whole game, my whole bag,
The ecstatic, terrifying flight itself,
Is wholly you -
My whole crazy world
Always,
Whatever.

STARTING A SONNET

Sometimes I sketch out a sonnet in 14 lines of free verse, and then wrestle it into organised shape with rhymes and rhythm, determined never to let the rhymes force me off-course. It is a terrible trial, and great fun. The poem might have 4 lines of statement or postulate, 8 lines of exposition and 2 lines of conclusion, or another permutation in the service of the story or polemic.

More commonly I begin with a good first line in pentameter, which inspires the rhyme for line 3; occasionally, lines 2 and 4 simply drop into place and I can move on to battle with the subsequent quatrains, eventually producing the first of many drafts in sonnet form. This is how I wrote WILD ORCHID.

***

I knew a woman as beautiful and rare as a wild orchid. She hated compliments, trusted no-one and refused affection. I saw, and worried, that she was lonelier with every year. I sent her WILD ORCHID, for which she thanked me graciously - but never understood that she was the subject...

16

WILD ORCHID

She unfurls her pearls to flirt with the sun, never knowing
Her wonder, envied, prized and desired by all;
Her secret speeds the heart, which starts, only slowing
With love-lost dreams come the dip to dead nightfall.
An unconscious call to us all, to the balls of a man,
Unknowing but bashful or brazen or both things in one,
Her beauty, full-blown and beguiling, bewitching, began
Like a pupa warm-batched, to be hatched, unmatched, in the sun.
Her slut-strutting twirl and her swirl are a skirl to the sky,
The bells of her buds babble moon-mute harmonious peals
That chime in the shell ears of angels all shimmering by,
Who must tumble and trip to the tunes with impossible squeals.

But stop the love-rich rains, let streams run dry,
Her wonder and her pride will surely die.

THE BAWDY SONNET

The Sonnet is a superb vehicle for filth. It is a shame that, in the 21st century, word games have been largely lost to the English language. As recently as the mid-20th century every schoolboy and most schoolgirls knew by memory the many bawdy verses of 'Twas on the Good Ship Venus. ("Twas on the good ship Venus, My God you should have seen us, The figurehead was a nude in bed, And the mast was the captain's penis...")

That is only a couple of generations ago, and already this great slice of culture has all but disappeared. Today, comedians use innuendo, of course, but, like punning, it is barely to be found in playground and street culture. In the Elizabethan age bawdy and scatological puns were part of what kept you chipper in hard times, cropping up routinely in songs and, of course, sonnets.

I NEED A CRAP, SAID JACK

I need a crap, said Jack, Oh fuck I do.

Well off you go, said Joe, Behind that wall,

Just squat right down, it's perfect for a poo,

There's leaves to wipe your bottom there and all.

But Jack came back. He said: I heard a sound,

I couldn't crap, although I did a wee,

A sort of clicking somewhere on the ground

That put the fucking fear of God in me.

Something you ate last night, maybe? said Joe.

I didn't eat at all last night! said Jack,

That clicking noise was why I couldn't go.

You haven't even had a fucking snack?

> Then I can tell you how this came to pass -
> It was your arse-cheeks snapping at the grass!

CRYPTIC SONNETS

The sonnet, organised and concise, is an especially good vehicle for the cryptic. I recommend Shakespeare's Sonnet 20 as an example, in which he worships the female beauty of a particular young man: "Which steals men's eyes and women's souls amazeth" = Which steels (hardens) men's eyes (the tip of the penis) and women's holes amazeth (makes maze-like when engorged). The hilarious sonnet is fun to unravel. Who was the "Hugh" in Shakespeare's world – indeed, was he implying more than one Hugh - to explain the contrived line: "A man in hue, all hues in his controlling"?

***

LINES TO TIME is a riddle.

In my poem, the dying poet is enjoying his last minutes on earth, indulgently constructing a complicated final poem about Inspiration and Destiny, and vaingloriously expecting Posterity to look after his memory with respect and admiration. He has almost finished the magnificent œuvre, and already has a final couplet in mind. Then the bloody phone rings.

Only one word suitably completes the twelfth line of the main stanza at the point of interruption. A clue: the poem is almost entirely iambic, so you are probably looking for a word of one syllable. My reader might guess it by checking the (complicated!) rhyming scheme ABCBAC; ABCBA?; DD...

LINES TO TIME

I drown;

Now beach my carcase on a sandy bed -
I'll wear it as a poet's carapace
Or siliqua, and sing immune to you,
You heart's-blood harrier. (A cinque-pace
Of disarmed rhythms captured in my head
Is chewing, chewing, chewing, chewing through:
O chew, trephining friends, for I am dead,
And water fills your oval prison space
Or theatre, and there is work to do,
You pretty pioneers.) Now on my face
And in the cryptic sand are splashes red -
A deadly, deadly, deadly, deadly…

TELEPHONE RINGS

You whipping, stripping bud-nipper, you swine,
You took my life and now you've killed my line.

SONNETS FOR TELLING STORIES

In ALL LOVED-UP AT THE HOLY SEPULCHRE (page 10), I use the sonnet form to tell a story as economically as possible without losing its humour.

Looking again at the poem I see there is also a bit of horror in there, though this is engendered more by the sinister atmosphere - the bony little priest in the hushed, shadowy stairwell of the Coptic chapel above the Holy Sepulchre - than by the assault itself. As a matter of interest, I discovered years later that a girl travelling with my brother in Israel had suffered a similar assault in the same place.

***

In 1994 I was commissioned as dramaturge to write the stage play for a production of Kafka's cruel masterpiece THE TRIAL at the Young Vic, London. The story is filled with horror, never less than in the scenes I describe in A WINTER TUESDAY KILL.

My sharp-eyed reader might spot that I have once again made it extra hard for myself with demanding, repeated conventions in the rhyming scheme.

The hapless K, inexplicably arrested, is no match for the implacable, merciless inquisitors of the State. During his trial he has a bizarre encounter with the beguiling Lenka (Leni); his fate is sealed...

Estelle's performance as Lenka was the sexiest thing I have ever seen on stage.

A WINTER TUESDAY KILL

(For Estelle, after Kafka)

Naked, through a spyhole in the door,

Lenka sees two men – one old, one young -

Crouching, draws a wrap up from the floor

And winds herself – the snare soon to be sprung -

In white, then lights a candle ritually.

Her carpet – such a pool of blue, such blue,

Which Lenka scarifies habitually

With circling toes as prisoned leopards do

The sawdust in their cages – changes hue,

Paling in the breathed-on waxy flame.

Now Lenka throws the bolt – as gaolers do,

Who carry all the keys but not the blame -

Well knowing why they came and what to say.

The older man presents his nephew K.

The lamping poacher's dog is tight to heel,

The rabbit's eyes are moons and filled with fright;

A blinding beam, a frozen target, real

Astonishment before the yellow bite -

And soil to sauce; a winter Tuesday kill.

A winter Tuesday still for Joseph K.

Sweet Lenka smells his blood but has no skill

To plead with eyes which see but cannot say,

"My Josef, run to see another day!"

For his are locked with hers on mutual schemes

And thus they freeze, and both are hunter's prey;

The poacher's hand is on their lashed-back dreams.

Not knowing what she wants or what to do,

Lenka blinks and shrinks away from view.

Now in her room again all blue, all blue,
Lenka slips her wrap and lets it fall,
And naked as a cat she stares anew
At sadness in a mirror on the wall.
The candle spits, and at her feet a moth
Is dying on a winter Tuesday night.
Mad Lenka with her toe teases the cloth
Towards the captive – scuffling, craving flight.

"Why such a death?" she whispers at the sight,
Treading the wrap with care to stop a life
Already stopped and hopeless in its fight,
"But any death is better than the knife."

Then knowing she must settle up a score,
She takes a plate and hurls it at the door.

For K, whose life depends on paper whims,

The evening's measured out in single files;

The lawyers drone, exoneration dims,

But Josef's blood is quick from Lenka's smiles.

Then Lenka's china, broken just for K,

Signals he must come; so, fixed as truth,

Though folded blind in dreams, he finds the way,

And logs the ledger of his life marked "Youth"

With Love's last sighting. Green, uncouth,

He stumbles from the room to Lenka's arms.

He does not hear his uncle's cry: "Forsooth,

He's fallen for that filthy trollop's charms!"

Only his sentence – deadlier than any –

Lenka's whispered: "You must call me Leni."

The "When - Then – But" SONNETS

We are often told that a sonnet should follow a classic format: 8 lines of postulate, 4 of exposition and 2 of conclusion. However, Shakespeare himself had a lot of fun shaping his sonnets with varying permutations. Three examples:

23 is 4 of postulate, 8 of exposition and 2 of conclusion.
73 is 3 quatrains of postulate and 2 of conclusion.

129 is worth looking at – in performance the quatrains can be usurped by an unstoppable rising crescendo without pause or obvious caesura, driving through 12 lines to a shattering climax. The conclusive final couplet can then be nailed home in the silence following - according to the performer's take on the poem: a resigned whisper, perhaps, a sob of frustration or a controlled statement.

The anti-climax is a wonderful weapon in oratory!

***

If a poem seems stuck on the runway, I recommend getting your first line down, setting out your When – Then – But format (or prepositions/subordinating conjunctions of your choice) and "filling the spaces", rhymes first.

THE ACTRESS AND THE PIRATE

When you bowled new-rigged across old Golden Square,
Some sultry Shakespeare temptress in your mind,
Your silken shift a mainsail, and your hair
A spinnaker all sluttish in the wind,
A taxi slowed, a driver crunched a gear,
A motorbike hard-braked, a tumbling hat,
A yuppy banker gawped, tabled his beer,
To whistles under breaths and "Look at that!",
Then pigeons wheeled like looney coastal birds
To welcome you, to escort you to your berth,
As, murmuring what I knew were William's words,
You served us all our rampant minds-eyes' worth.

But I had met the nomad in your eyes,
And now I swore that you would be my prize.

3 FREE-VERSE POEMS WHICH ALMOST BECAME SONNETS

SOFT LANDINGS, HEDGE-CUTTING IN 48 DEGREES and LANDSCAPE PAINTER AT DUSK are of course not classic sonnets. I include them in this collection because all three are trains of thought fully expressed and resolved in fourteen lines – sonnets in all but rhyme. In all three cases I actually set out to write a sonnet, but my pen took me down another road.

My reader is welcome either to pretend they are not here, or to indulge me and classify the three poems as "free-verse sonnets".

***

When Country Life Magazine accepted SOFT LANDINGS for publication, the editor asked me if I would improve the title. The poem is about lovemaking. It begins quietly and intimately, builds rhythmically to a climax and finishes with 2 lines of anti-climax, when the exploded seeds come softly to land on earth. Believing that the poem had most likely been approved for publication as a "Nature" poem, with acceptably modest references to agricultural bounty and fertility, I changed the title to THE GREEN AGE rather than lose the sale on account of the title.

SOFT LANDINGS

In a giggling, whiskery tissue of a minute,

When shelled, tip-tongued consonants pink and bill,

When all the world breathes deep and voiceless,

When lips sow tender, popping pips,

And white downy downs shoo-shoo like stroked velvet,

Then magic hills sidle and press, merge,

And milk a common root, a gland, a tap,

A loving, ever-suckling source of sweet juice,

And burgeon, blossom, blow a catherine wheel,

Their anthem, their tossed fruits, skyward,

Which – spinning, singing, falling, random,

Whimsical, exact, plum in the middle,

Parachuting peace-boys, bulls-eyeing seed bullets -

Tease the silly world with airy whispers and soft landings.

In LANDSCAPE PAINTER AT DUSK, my subject is an artist – an old, old artist. He has repeated himself time and again over the long years, exploring always the same themes, the same colours, the same angers, the same wretched pleasures...

Has he become a cliché of himself? That is his fear. He is blocked. Inspiration will not come. His palette is dry. His brush is atrophied in his hand. His beloved landscapes have turned on him, vengefully.

This could kill him...

LANDSCAPE PAINTER AT DUSK

Earth turns.

The Master considers.

His landscape, concussed at dusk after visitors,
Horizontal disturbance, rape, is dizzy:
In whirling yards on mobile hills the wind
Punishes small things privately.

His stillness belies great revolutions;
Earth turns through him, a spinning wheel,
Spokes, spikes, spires thrash clouds,
Plundered chambers swung in furling hollows
Charge the wind, the web, spin the senseless
Centrifugal strings; a million mullioned
Hooping meadows, mad with whipping, blur,
Bleach the spectrum – freeze the fulcrum.

Fatefully, centrally fixed, itching for force,
His mind screws still, still in the wheel.

Sometimes a poem roars out of you like a wild animal released from captivity. At these times it does not pay to try shackling the thing with form, though for everyone's safety a decent boundary fence must be in place, leaving enough paddock for the poem to work off its frustration at containment, without allowing it to become a danger to the community.

My decent boundary fence in the case of HEDGECUTTING IN 48 DEGREES was the fourteen line limit. Under such circumstances I do not hunt for rhymes or restrictive meter, but nonetheless like to consider the poem a sonnet. I was even briefly tempted to use "to the floor" instead of "with his catch" to give me a rhyming couplet sign-off – but "catch" was the word, "catch" was the thought - and it stayed!

***

I have lived in the South of France for many years. During the very hot summer of 2018 I was stung furiously by a wasp I had disturbed while shaping a 4-metre high pyracantha hedge just after lunch. Yes: Mad dogs and Englishmen... That day, the temperature in the full shade of the canopied mulberries up by the house reached a record 48 degrees Celsius. It was a Saharan day. Down in the field where I was working, there was no shade.

I was lucky my sniper was a lone wasp, as I had enraged dozens, their nest only inches inside the hedge. I was wearing a long work shirt - an old black- and green-sleeved shell top I had selected for protection.

The tiny soldier stung me, painfully, right through my shirt, his sting like a white-hot surgical tool, drilled perfectly into the centre of my neurological plexus, it seemed, by some demonic acupuncturist...

HEDGE-CUTTING IN 48 DEGREES

The old, torn shell top, worn against the wasps,
Was stuck to his wet, stung back like a crayfish's shell,
Nailed. He was bent double, an old, stung crayfish, wild,
Hauling at his old, stuck, soaking, torn shell, shouting, cursing,
Shot, stung, targeted, sniped, stuck, soaked,
The screaming trimmer jangling down, the shell in fist,
The old crayfish shedding, grasping, swearing, tearing,
Hauling, mauling, bawling, fists and elbows flailing,
Stuck, drenched - when suddenly it rolled brutal over his head,
A drenched rope hauled in from the brutal brine, smack,
Rasping and rough as rope, salty, rasping his neck,
Roughing his right ear, his scalp, a salty sling, smack -
And like an old salt, drenched, he slumped back with his catch,
Stung and wild, soaked, slumped, hurt, cursing some more.

Towards the end of 1977 a tree was planted in my honour in the Shalom Forest, Jerusalem. It was designated tree number 1466 AB. I have the citation to this day. It was a good time to be in Jerusalem - a time of reconciliation and hope.

After Israel's most deliberately planned, genocidal assault on Gaza in 2014, targeting hospitals, shelters and schools, destroying 20,000 homes, displacing 500,000 residents and killing more than 2,000 Palestinians including nearly 500 children, I was furious, and wrote many poems in my rage. About 70 Israelis died in the conflict.

I wanted to go back to Jerusalem and haul that innocent tree right out by the roots...

BITTER UNTIL CURED

The betrayed heart and the olive –
Both are bitter until cured.
Little olive tree, I hate you.

I would bomb you, little tree, tonight,
Strafe your flailing roots and leafless bones,
Then, if still there all brave in morning's light,
I'd shell you hard from several circling drones,
Your baby olives bouncing on the ground,
Too green to seed, too smashed, I would not care;
I'd fry your roots and bulldoze all around,
And boil your sap and nose the rancid air,
For vintage notes of death that might transport
The arboricidal connoisseur to Heaven,
And recognise the year and shout, cavort –
The eighth of December, nineteen seventy-seven!
      The end, to be sure, of this important tree:
      Number fourteen sixty-six A-B.

The betrayed heart and the olive –
Both are bitter until cured.
Little olive tree, I love you.

I would touch you, little tree, embrace
Your noble trunk and love each twinkling star
That dots your fanning canopy of lace –
And those that splash night's iron dome as far
As helplessness across the desert sands,
To Gaza, rubbled, razed and robbed of hope,
Where skulls are flowers and weeds are broken hands –
But love the world that promised life and scope,
Then tore the seedlings from the nursery pot
Where daily nourishment was guaranteed,
Transplanted them and said that was their lot,
Imprisoned them in walls of concrete screed?
    Oh, nothing is your fault, my little tree,
     For you are just a pawn of history.

The betrayed heart and the olive –
Both are bitter until cured.
Little olive tree, my olive tree.

A sonnet is the ideal medium for saying a succinct and heartfelt thank you.

FRIENDSHIP IN A JAR OF BEANS

(For Claire)

Oh they'll tell you in platitudes what friendship means,

They'll swear, my dearest friend, there's nothing better,

They'll prove it with a coffee or jar of beans,

They'll promise you the earth in a loving letter,

They'll whisper friends are there, just like the stars,

They'll smile there's just one mind for a pair of hearts,

They'll vow together you can heal the scars,

They'll seem to worship you and all your parts,

They'll say it doubles your joys, divides your grief,

They'll suggest you seek it in the little things,

They'll find it in a flower or glinting leaf,

They'll share your heartbeat when the nightbird sings;

      But when the chips are down and all seems bare,

      That's when they go - and you, dear friend, are there.

... POSTSCRIPT ...

Few poets are bothering with sonnets these days. More's the pity. If this little book has encouraged you to express yourself in fourteen structured lines, I am happy – and should love to see the results.

France January 2019

Printed in Poland
by Amazon Fulfillment
Poland Sp. z o.o., Wrocław

53304772R00033